Beuys is Boys

A Guide to the Pronunciation of Artists, Architects, Works of Art, Museums and More...

by
Susan Ford

ISBN: 978-1-877675-73-7

Midmarch Arts Press
300 Riverside Drive
New York, NY 10025

1st Printing   2008
2nd Printing   2010

Contents

Introduction

This pronunciation guide to artists' names, works of art, foreign museums and terms is as straightforward and easily comprehensible as possible. Few symbols are utilized and there are no obscure schemes to grapple with. Just enunciate each syllable as indicated and you've got it. If asked to repeat the name, say it again, even louder. Say it with confidence because you know you are correct and that it is the listener's version of the name that is questionable.

Mispronunciations heard over a short period of time on a respected national radio station were the inspiration for this guide: Cimabue was anglicized, Dürer was frenchified, Malevich was mangled and Modigliani was once again just malpronounced. Since this project began there have been many other similar instances indicating *Beuys is Boys* will appeal to a wide and varied audience.

Those who will benefit from this guide range from art lovers to the newly initiated, from respected academics to the humblest students, from museum directors and personnel to the casual visitor, virtually anyone interested in art (even those who aren't, but wish, or must, refer to an artist's name, terminology, foreign museum, or work of art).

Rather than producing a mind-boggling list of hundreds of names, many of which would be quite obscure, we have included only ones that the reader is the most likely to encounter. All names of English origin are also excluded, unless problematic, as this guide is intended specifically for American readers. In addition, architects, photographers and designers are listed along with the painters and sculptors.

Just a few notations:

Stress: The stress in the name is indicated in bold face. It is important to remember that there is *no* stress in French words: each syllable receives equal emphasis (the same applies to Japanese).

Muted Consonants: In French the final letter of the word is usually mute. Exceptions are C, F, L and R.

Symbols/Sounds

Guttural Consonants: ḵ

There is no English equivalent for the German and Dutch "ch". It is a guttural 'k'. We have, therefore indicated it with a "ḵ' (as in k with a kick).

Nasal vowels: '(n)'

There is also no English equivalent for the French nasal sound. Say the vowel as if you nose were plugged or you were holding your nose. We have therefore, indicated it with an '(n)' (as in n for nose enclosed).

Now go and enjoy looking at those works by Cimabue, Pollaiuolo, Dieric Bouts, Vuillard, Modigliani, Atget, Moholy-Nagy, Rusha, and the Wassily Chair by Breuer...

(chee-mah-**boo**-eh, pohl-lah-**yoh**-loh, deerk bowts, vwee-yahr, moh-deel-**yah**-nee, aht-zhay, **moh**-hoh-lee **nahj**, roo-**shay** and the vah-**see**-lee chair by **broh**-yuhr)...

Artists A - Z

Aalto, Alvar
Finnish Architect
1900-1947

ahl-toh, al-vahr

Alberti, Leon Battista
Italian Architect
1404-1472

ahl-**bair**-tee

Alechinsky, Pierre
Belgian Painter
1927-

ah-luh-**shin**-skee

Alma-Tadema, Lawrence
English (b. Holland) Painter
1836-1912

al-mah **tah**-deh-mah

Andrea del Castagno
Italian Painter
act. 1442-d.145

ahn-**dreh**-ah dehl
kahs-**tahn**-yoh

Angelico, Fra
Italian Painter
act. c.1417- d.1455

ahn-**jeh**-lee-koh

Appel, Karel
Dutch Painter
1921 -

ahp-ulh

Arbus, Diane
American Photographer
1923-1971

ahr-buhs, dee-**ann**

Arcimboldo, Giuseppe
Italian Painter
c.1530-1593

ahr-cheem-**bohl**-doh

Archipenko, Alexander
American (b. Ukraine) Sculptor
1887-1964

ahr-kee-**peng**-koh

Atget, Eugène
French Photographer
1857-1927

aht-zhay

Aulenti, Gae
Italian Architect
1927-

ow-**lehn**-tee, guy

Avedon, Richard
American Photographer
1923-2004

ave-eh-don

Baj, Enrico
Italian Painter
1924-200

b(eye)

Bakst, Leon
Russian Painter
1866-1924

baxt

Balla, Giacomo
Italian Painter
1871-1958

bahl-lah

Balthus
(Balthazar Klossowski)
French Painter
1908-2001

bahl-tewz

Barlach, Ernst
German Sculptor
1870-1938

bahr-lahş

Barye, Antoine-Louis
French Sculptor
1796-1875

bah-ree

Baselitz, Georg
German Artist
1939-

bah-seh-litz

Basquiat, Jean-Michel
American Painter
1960-1988

bahs-**kee**-aht

Bassano, Jacopo
Italian Painter
act. c.1535-d.1592

bah-**sah**-noh

Baumeister, Willi
German Painter
1889-1955

bow-m(eye)-ster
(as in cow)

Baziotes, William
American Painter
1912-1963

bahz-ee-**oh**-teez

Becher, Bernd
German Photographer
1931-

beh<u>k</u>-uhr

Beckman, Max
German Painter
1884-1955

beck-mahn

Bellini, Giovanni
Italian Painter
act. c.1459-d.1516

behl-**lee**-nee

Berlage, Henrik Petrus
Dutch Architect
1856-1934

behr-lah-guh

Bernini, Giovanni Lorenzo
Italian Architect
1598-1680

bair-**nee**-nee

Bertoia, Harry
American Sculptor/Designer
1915-1978

bair-**toy**-ah

Beuys, Joseph
German Artist
1921-1986

boys

Bierstadt, Albert
American (b. Germany) Painter
1830-1902

beer-shtat

Birkerts, Gunner
American (b. Latvia) Architect
1925-

buhr-kehrts, **goo**-nehr
(Correct in North America)

Boccioni, Umberto
Italian Painter/Sculptor
1882-1916

boht-**choh**-nee

5

Bonheur, Rosa
French Painter
1822-1899

boh(n)-uhr

Bonnard, Pierre
French Painter
1867-1947

boh-nahr

Bontecou, Lou
American Sculptor
1931-

bawn-tuh-koo

Borduas, Paul-Émile
Canadian Painter
1905-1960

bohr-dwah

Borromini, Francesco
Italian Architect
1599-1667

boh-roh-**mee**-nee

Bosch, Hieronymus
Dutch Painter
c.1450-1516

bahsh
(Popular and acceptable,
'boss' is actually correct)

Botticelli, Sandro
Italian Painter
1444/45-1510

boht-tee-**chel**-lee

Boucher, François
French Painter
1703-1770

boo-shay

Boudin, Eugène
French Painter
1824-1898

boo-dah(n)

Bouguereau, Adolphe-William
French Painter
1825-1905

boo-guh-roh

Boullée, Étienne-Louis
French Architect
1728-1799

bool-lay

Bourgeois, Louise
American (b. France) Sculptor
1911-

boor-zhwah

Bouts, Dieric
Flemish Painter
act. c.1420-d.1475

bowts, deerk

Bramante, Donato
Italian Architect
1444-1514

brah-**mahn**-tay

Brancusi, Constantin
Romanian Sculptor
1876-1957

brahn-**koo**-zee

Braque, Georges
French Painter
1882-1963

brahk

Brassaï
(Gyula Halàsz)
French (b. Hungary) Photographer
1899-1984

brah-s(eye)

Breuer, Marcel
American Architect
1902-1981

broy-yuhr

Bruegel, Pieter(the Elder)
Flemish Painter
act. c. 1551- d.1569

broy-guhl
(Many variations. This quite acceptable)

Bruggen, Coosje van
Dutch/American Sculptor
1942

broo-gun, **koh**-sha vahn

Brunelleschi, Filippo
Italian Architect
1377-1446

broo-neh-**lehs**-kee

Buffet, Bernard
French Painter
1928-

bew-fay

Buren, Daniel
French Artist
1938-

bew-rah(n)

Caillebotte, Gustave
French Painter
1848-1894

k(eye)-uh-boht

Calatrava, Santiago
Spanish Architect
1951-

kah-lah-**trah**-vah

Calder, Alexander
American Sculptor
1898-1976

kawl-duhr

Canaletto
(Giovanni Antonio Canal)
Italian Painter
1697-1768

kah-nah-**leht**-toh

Caravaggio
(Michelangelo Merisi da)
Italian Painter
1573-1610

kah-rah-**vah**-djoh

Carpeaux, Jean Baptiste   kar-poh
French Sculptor
1827-1875

Carracci, Annibale   kah-rah-chee
Italian Painter
1560-1609

Cartier-Bresson, Henri   kahr-tyay bruh-so(n)
French Photographer
1908-2004

Cassatt, Mary   kass-satt
American Painter
1845-1926

Cellini, Benvenuto   chel-ee-nee
Italian Sculptor
1500-1571

Cézanne, Paul   say-zann
French Painter
1839-1906

Chagall, Marc   shah-gahl
French (b. Russia) Painter
1887-1985

Chardin, Jean Baptiste
French Painter
1699-1779

shar-da(n)

Chihuly, Dale
American Glass Artist
1941-

chih-**hoo**-lee

Chirico, Giorgio de
Italian Painter
1888-1978

kee-ree-koh

Christo
(Christo Javacheff)
American (b. Bulgaria) Artist
1935-

kris-toh

Christus, Petrus
Flemish Painter
act. c. 1444-d.1475/76

kree-stuhss

Cimabue
(Cenni di Pepe)
Italian Painter
c.1240-1302

chee-mah-**boo**-weh

Clouet, Jean
French Painter
act. c.1516-d.1541

kloo-ay

Cocteau, Jean
French Artist
1889-1963

kohk-toh

Corot, Jean-Baptiste
French Painter
1796-1875

koh-roh

Correggio
(Antonio Allegri)
Italian Painter
act. c.1514-d.1534

koh-**red**-jioh

Courbet, Gustave
French Painter
1819-1877

koor-bay

Coysevox, Antoine
French Sculptor
1640-1720

kwah-zuh-voh

Cranach, Lucas
German Painter
1472-1553

krah-nah<u>k</u>

Cuyp, Aelbert
Dutch Painter
1620-1691

k(eye)p

Daguerre, Louis-Jacques
French Photographer
1787-1851

dah-gehr

Dalí, Salvador
Spanish Painter
1904-1989

dah-**lee**
(Correct. Many misplace
stress as in **dah**-lee)

**Daubigny, Charles
François**
French Painter
1817-1878

doh-been-yee

Daumier, Honoré
French Painter
1808-1879

doh-myay

David, Jacques-Louis
French Painter
1748-1825

dah-veed

Degas, Edgar
French Painter/Sculptor
1834-1917

duh-gah *
(Correct. Many give improper
stress as in **day**-gah)

De Kooning, Willem
American (b. Netherlands) Painter
1904-1997

duh **koo**-ning

Delacroix, Eugène
French Painter
1798-1863

duh-lah-krwah

Delaunay, Robert
French Painter
1885-1941

duh-loh-nay

Della Robbia, Luca
Italian Sculptor
1399-1482

del-lah **rohb**-bee-ah

Delvaux, Paul
Belgian Painter
1897-1994

del-voh

Demuth, Charles
American Painter
1883-1935

deh-**mooth**

Derain, André
French Painter
1880-1954

duh-ra(n)

Diebenkorn, Richard
American Painter
1922-1993

dee-ben-kohrn

Dine, Jim
American Artist
1935-

d(eye)n

Doesburg, Theo van
Dutch Painter
1883-1931

dooz-berg

Doisneau, Robert
French Photographer
1912-1994

dwah-noh

Domenico Veneziano

Italian Painter
act. 1438-1461

doh-**may**-nee-koh
vehn-ay-tsee-**ah**-noh

Donatello
(Donato di Niccolo)
Italian Sculptor
1386-1466

dohn-ah-**tehl**-oh

Doré, Gustav
French Artist
1832-1883

doh-ray

Dubuffet, Jean
French Painter
1901-1985

dew-boo-fay

Duccio
(Duccio di Buoninsegna)
Italian Painter
c. 1255-1319

doo-choh

Duchamp, Marcel
French Painter/Sculptor
1887-1968

dew-sha(n)

Dufy, Raoul
French Painter
1877-1953

dew-fee

Dughet, Gaspard
French (b. Italy) Painter
1615-1675

dew-gay

Dürer, Albrecht
German Painter
1471-1528

dew-ruhr

Dyck, Anton van
Flemish Painter
1599-1641

d(eye)k

Erté
(Romain de Tirtoff)
Russian/French Designer
1892-1990

ehr-tay

Eyck, Jan van
Flemish Painter
act. c.1422-d.1441

(eye)k

Fantin-Latour, Henri
French Painter
1836-1904

fah(n)-ta(n) lah-toor

Feininger, Lyonel
American Painter
1871-1956

f(**eye**)-ning-uhr

Fischl, Eric
American Painter, Sculptor
1948-

fee-shuhl

Flavin, Dan
American Artist
1933-1966

flay-vin

Flémalle, Master of
Flemish Painter
1614-1675

flay-mahl

Fortuny, Mariano
Spanish Designer
1871-1949

fohr-**too**-nee

Fouquet, Jean
French Painter
1420-1481

foo-kay

Fragonard, Jean-Honoré
French Painter
1732-1806

frah-goh-nahr

Fuseli, Henry
Swiss (act. England) Painter
1741-1825

fyoo-zuh-lee

Gabo, Naum
American (b. Russia) Sculptor
1890-1977

gah-boh, nowm

Gabriel, Ange-Jacques
French Architect
1698-1782

gah-bree-uhl

Gallé, Émile
French Glassmaker
1846-1904

gahl-lay

Garnier, Charles
French Architect
1825-1898

gahr-nyay

Gaudi, Antonio
Spanish Architect
1852-1926

gow-dee

Gauguin, Paul
French Painter
1848-1903

goh-ga(n)

Gehry, Frank
American Architect
1929-

gair-ee

Gentile da Fabriano
Italian Painter
act. c.1408-d.1427

jen-**tee**-lay dah
fahb-ree-**yah**-noh

Gentileschi, Artemisia
Italian Painter
1593-1651/52

jen-tee-**lehs**-kee

Géricault, Théodore
French Painter
1791-1824

zhay-ree-koh

Ghiberti, Lorenzo
Italian Sculptor
1378-1455

ghee-**bair**-tee

Ghirlandaio, Domenico
Italian Painter
1449-1494

gheer-lahn-**d(eye)**-oh

Giacometti, Alberto
Swiss Sculptor, Painter
1901-1966

jah-koh-**meh**-tee

Giorgione
(Giorgio del Castelfranco)
Italian Painter
c.1478-1510

johr-**joh**-neh

Giotto
(Giotto di Bondone)
Italian Painter
1266/67-1337

joht-toh

Gleize, Albert
French Painter
1881-1953

glehz

Gogh, Vincent van
Dutch Painter
1853-1890

van-goh
(Stick with this.
 Many variations)

Gossaert, Jan
Flemish Painter
act. 1503-d.1532

gaw-**sahrt**

Goya, Francisco
Spanish Painter
1746-1828

goy-ah

Gozzoli, Benozzo
Italian Painter
c.1420-d.1497

goht-**soh**-lee

Greco, El
(Domenikos Theotocopoulos)
Greek (act. Spain) Painter
1541-1614

ell **grehk**-koh

Greuze, Jean-Baptiste
French Painter
1725-1805

grewz

Gris, Juan
Spanish (act.France) Painter
1887-1927

gree
(Prefered by author.
Properly: 'grees')

Gropius, Walter
German/American Architect
1883-1969

groh-pee-us

Grosz, George
German/American Painter
1893-1957

grohss

Grünewald, Matthias
German Painter
c.1470-d.1528

grew-nuh-vahlt

Guardi, Francesco
Italian Painter
1712-1793

gwahr-dee

Guimard, Hector
French Architect
1867-1942

ghee-mahr

Guys, Constantin
French Painter
1805-1892

ghees

Haacke, Hans
German (act NY) Artist
1936-

haa-kuh

Hadid, Zaha
London-based (b. Beirut) Architect
1950-

hah-**deed, zah**-hah

Hals, Frans
Dutch Painter
c.1580?-d.1666

hahls

Hassam, Childe
American Painter
1859-1935

hass-ahm, child

Haussmann, Georges Eugène
French Urban Designer
1809-1891

ows- mahn
(as in cows)

Hejduk, John
American Architect
1929-2000

hey-dook

Hine, Lewis
American Photographer
1874-1940

h(eye)n

Hiroshige, Ando
Japanese Printmaker
1797-1858

hir-oh-shee-gay

Hobbema, Meindert
Dutch Painter
1638-1709

hob-buh-mah

Höch, Hannah
German Painter
1889-1978

hoeck

Hokusai, Katsushika
Japanese Printmaker
1760-1849

hoh-k-s(eye)

Holbein, Hans
German Painter
1497-1543

hohl-b(eye)n

Hooch, Pieter de
Dutch Painter
1629-1684

hohkh

Hundertwasser, Friedensreich
(Friedrich Stowasser)
Austrian Painter
1928-2000

hoon-dert-vah-sehr

Ingres, Jean-Auguste-Dominique
French Painter
1780-1867

a(n)-gruh

Isozaki, Arata
Japanese Architect
1931-

ee-soh-za-kee

Jahn, Helmut
American Architect
1940-

yahn

Jawlensky, Alexei van
Russian Painter
1867-1941

yah-**vlen**-skee

Jekyll, Gertrude
English Garden Designer
1843-1932

jhee-kuhl
(as in treacle)

Jongkind, Johan Barthold
Dutch Painter
1819-1891

yohng-kint

Jordaens, Jacob
Flemish Painter
1593-1678

yohr-dahns

Jorn, Asger
Danish Painter
1914-1973

yawrn

Kandinsky, Wassily
Russian Painter
1866-1944

kahn-**din**-skee

Kertész, André
American (b. Hungary) Photographer
1894-1985

kehr-tesh

Kienholz, Edward
American Artist
1927-1994

keen-hohlts

Kirchner, Ernst Ludwig
German Painter
1880-1938

kihrş-nuhr

Kitaj, R.B.
American (act. England) Painter
1932-

kee-**tazh**

Klee, Paul
German (Swiss) Painter
1879-1940

klay

Klimt, Gustav
Austrian Painter
1862-1918

klimt

Kokoschka, Oskar
Austrian Painter
1886-1980

koh-**kosh**-kah

Kollwitz, Käthe
German Painter, Printmaker
1867-1945

kohl-vits

Koolhaas, Rem
Dutch Architect
1944-

kool-hahss

Krieghoff, Cornelius
Canadian Painter
1815-1872

kreeg-hawf

Lachaise, Gaston
American (b. France) Sculptor
1882-1935

lah- shehz

La Fresnaye, Roger de
French Painter
1885-1925

lah fray-nay

Lalique, René
French Glassmaker
1860-1945

lah-leek

Lam, Wifredo
Cuban (act. France) Artist
1902-1982

lahm

Le Corbusier
(Charles Eduard Jeanneret)
French Architect
1887-1965

luh kohr-bew-zyay

Ledoux, Claude Nicholas
French Architect
1736-1806

luh-doo

Leduc, Ozias
Canadian Painter
1864-1955

luh-dewk

Léger, Fernand
French Painter
1881-1955

lay-zhay

Lehmbruck, Wilhelm
German Sculptor
1881-1919

laym-brook

Lempicka, Tamara di
American (b. Poland) Painter
1898-1980

lehm-**pee**-ka

Le Nain, Antoine
French Painter
c.1588-1648

luh na(n)

Le Nôtre, André
French Landscape Architect
1613-1700

luh noh-truh

Leonardo da Vinci
Italian Painter
1452-1519

leh-oh-**nahr**-doh
dah **vin**-chee

Le Sidaner, Henri
French Painter
1862-1939

luh-see-da(n)-yay

Lhote, André
French Painter
1885-1962

loht

Lichtenstein, Roy
American Painter, Sculptor
1923-1997

lihk-tuhn-st(eye)n

Lipchitz, Jacques
French (b. Lithuania) Sculptor
1891-1973

lihp-shits

Lippi, Fra Filippo
Italian Painter
c.1406-d.1469

lip-pee

Lissitzky, El(iezer)
Russian Painter
1890-1941

lih-**sits**-kee

Loos, Adolf
Austrian Architect
1870-1933

lohss

Lorrain, Claude
French Painter
1604/5?-1682

loh-ra(n)

Lurçat, Jean
French Painter, Designer
1892-1966

lewr-sah

Lutyens, Edward
English Architect
1869-1944

lut-yenz
(as in but)

Macke, August
German Painter
1887-1914

ma-kuh

Maes, Nicholaes
Dutch Painter
1634-1693

mahs

Magritte, René
Belgian Painter
1898-1967

mah-greet

Maillart, Robert
Swiss Architect
1872-1940

mah-yahr

Maillol, Aristide
French Sculptor
1861-1944

mah-yoll

Malevich, Kazimir
Russian Painter
1878-1935

mah-lay-vich

Manet, Édouard
French Painter
1832-1883

mah-nay

Mansart, Jules Hardouin
French Architect
1645-1708

ma(n)-sahr

Mantegna, Andrea
Italian Painter
act. 1441/5-d.1506

mahn-teh-nyah

Mapplethorpe, Robert
American Photographer
1946-1982

may-pul-thorp

Marin, John
American Painter
1870-1953

mar-ihn

Marisol
(Marisol Escobar)
Venezuelan Sculptor
1930-

mah-ree-sohl

Marquet, Albert
French Sculptor
1875-1947

mar-kay

Masaccio
(Tomasso di Giovanni)
Italian Painter
1401-1428

mah-**zaht**-choh

Massys, Quentin
Flemish Painter
1465/6-1530

mah-**sees**

Mathieu, George
French Painter
1921-

ma-tyuh

Matisse, Henri
French Painter
1869-1954

mah-teess

Mau, Bruce
Canadian designer
1959-

mow
(as in how)

Meier, Richard
American Archhitect
1934-

m(eye)-uhr

Meissonier, Ernest
French Painter
1815-1891

mehs-sohn-yay

Michelangelo Buonarroti
Italian Painter, Sculptor, Architect
1475-1564

m(eye)kehl-**ahn**-
jeh-loh   (Popular.
Correct 'mee'-kehl)

Mies van der Rohe, Ludwig
German/American Architect
1886-1969

mees van duh **roh**-uh

Millais, John Everett
English Painter
1829-1896

mih-lay

Millet, Jean-François
French Painter
1814-1875

mee-lay

Miró, Joan
Spanish Painter, Sculptor
1893-1983

mee-**roh**

Modigliani, Amadeo
Italian Painter, Sculptor
1884-1920

moh-deel-**yah**-nee

Moholy-Nagy, László
American (b. Hungary) Artist
1895-1946

moh-hoh-lee-**nah**-juh

Mondrian, Piet
Dutch Painter
1872-1944

mohn-dree-ahn

Moneo, Raphael
Spanish Architect
1937-

moh-**nay**-oh

Monet, Claude
French Painter
1840-1926

moh-nay

Moreau, Gustav
French Painter
1741-1814

moh-roh

Morisot, Berthe
French Painter
1841-1895

moh-ree-zoh

Morrice, James Wilson
Canadian Painter
1865-1944

moh-reess

Mucha, Alphonse
Czech Painter
1860-1939

muhk-ah

Munch, Edvard
Norwegian Painter
1863-1944

muhngk

Muybridge, Eadweard
American (b. England) Photographer
1830-1904

moy-bridge

Nadar
(Gaspard-Felix Tournachon)
French Photographer
1820-1910

nah-dahr

Nattier, Jean-Marc
French Painter
1685-1766

na-tyay

Nauman, Bruce
American Artist
1940-

now-mahn

Neutra, Richard
Austrian (act. U.S) Architect
1892-1970

noy-trah

Newman, Barnett
American Painter
1905-1970

noo-muhn

Niemeyer, Oscar
Brazilian Architect
1907-

nee-m(eye)-ehr

Noguchi, Isamu
American Sculptor, Designer
1904-1988

noh-**goo**-chee

Nolde, Emil
German Painter
1867-1956

nohl-duh

Oldenburg, Claes
American (b. Sweden) Sculptor
1929-

old-en-berg, klahss

Orcagna, Andrea
Italian Painter,Sculptor
act. c.1343-d.1368

ohr-**kahn**-yah

Ozenfant, Amédée
French Painter
1886-1966

oh-zah(n)-fah(n)

Palladio, Andrea
Italian Architect
1508-1580

pah-**lah**-dee-oh

Paolozzi, Eduardo
English (b. Scotland) Sculptor
1924-

pah-oh-**loht**-see

Parmigianino, Francesco
Italian Painter
1503-1540

pahr-mee-jiah-**nee**-
noh

Pascin, Jules
American (b. Bulgaria) Painter
1885-1930

pahs-keen*
(*Often Frenchified
to 'pahs-ka[n]')

Pei, I.M.
American (b. China) Architect
1917-

pay

Pereira, Irene Rice
American Painter
1907-1971

puh-**ray**-ruh

Perugino, Pietro
Italian Painter
act. c.1472-d.1523

peh-roo-**jhee**-noh

Pesce, Gaetano
Italian Architect, Designer
1939-

pey-sheh

Picasso, Pablo
Spanish (act. France) Painter
1881-1973

pee-**kahs**-soh

Piero della Francesca

Italian Painter
c.1415/20-1492

pee-**eh**-roh deh-la
frahn-**chess**-kah

Piranesi, Giovanni Battista
Italian Engraver
1720-1778

pee-rah-**nay**-zee

Pisanello
(Antonio Pisano)
Italian Painter
act. c.1415-c.1455

pee-zah-**nehl**-loh

Pissarro, Camille
French Painter
1830-1903

pee-sah-roh

Plecnik, Joseph
Czechoslovakian Architect
1872-1957

pletch-neek

Poiret, Paul
French Designer
1879-1944

pwah-ray

Pollaiuolo, Antonio
Italian Sculptor,Painter
c.1457-d.1498

pohl-lay-**yioh**-loh

Portzamparc, Christian de
French Architect
1944-

pohr-zahm-pahrk

Poussin, Nicolas
French Painter
1615-1675

poo-sa(n)

Prouvé, Jean
French Designer, Architect
1901-1984

proo-vay

Putman, Andrée
French Architect, Designer
1934(?) -

pewt-ma(n)

Puvis de Chavannes, Pierre
French Painter
1824-1898

pew-vee duh sha-van

Quercia, Jacopo della
Italian Sculptor
c.1371-74 - d.1438

kwehr-chah

Quesnel, François
French Painter
c.1543/44-1616

kay-nehl

Raphael
(Raffaello Sanzio)
Italian Painter
1483-1520

rah-fah-ehl

Rauschenberg, Robert
American Artist
1925-

row-shuhn-buhrg
(as in cow)

Redon, Odilon
French Painter
1814-1916

ruh-da(n)

Rembrandt van Rijn
Dutch Painter
1606-1669

rehm-brahnt

Renoir, Pierre-August
French Painter
1841-1919

rehn-wahr

Ribera, Jusepe de
Spanish Painter
1588-1652

ree-**bay**-rah

Richter, Gerhard
German Artist
1932-

rihk-tuhr

Riemenschneider, Tilman
German Sculptor
c. 1460-1531

ree-mehn-shn(eye)-duhr

Rietveld, Gerrit
Dutch Architect, Designer
1888-1964

reet-velt

Rigaud, Hyacinth
French Painter
1659-1743

ree-goh

Riis, Jacob
American Photographer
1849-1914

reess

Riopelle, Jean-Paul
Canadian Painter
1923-2002

ree-oh-pehl

Rivera, Diego
Mexican Painter
1886-1957

ree-**vay**-rah

Rodchenko, Alexander
Russian Painter, Photographer
1891-1956

rod-**cheng**-koh

Rodin, Auguste
French Sculptor
1814-1917

roh-dah(n)

Rossetti, Dante Gabriel
English Painter
1828-1882

roh-**set**-tee

Roth, Dieter
German/Swiss Artist
1930-1998

roht, **dee**-tehr

Rousseau, Henri
French Painter
1844-1910

roo-soh

Rouault, Georges
French Painter
1871-1958

roo-oh

Rubens, Peter Paul
Flemish Painter
1577-1640

roo-behnz

Ruhlmann, Jacques-Émile
French Designer
1879-1933

rool-mahn

Ruisdale, Jacob von
Dutch Painter
1600-1670

roys-dahl

Ruscha, Edward
American Painter, Photographer
1937-

roo-**shay**

Saarinen, Eero
Finnish/American Architect
1910-1961

sahr-ihn-uhn, air-oh

Saint Phalle, Niki de
French Painter, Sculptor
1930-2002

sa(n) fahl

Samaras, Lucas
American (b. Greece) Artist
1936-

sah-**mah**-ruhs

Schiele, Egon
Austrian Painter
1890-1918

shee-luh

Schinkel, Karl Friedrich
German Architect
1781-1841

shihn-kuhl

Schnabel, Julian
American Painter
1951-

shnah-buhl

Schwitters, Kurt
German Painter, Sculptor
1887-1948

shvit-tuhrs

Segal, George
American Sculptor
1924-2000

see-guhl

Seghers, Gerard
Flemish Painter
1591-1651

zay-guhrs

Seurat, Georges
French Painter
1859-1891

suh-rah

Signac, Paul
French Painter
1863-1935

seen-yak

Signorelli, Luca
Italian Painter
c.1445/50-1523

see-nyoh-**rel**-lee

Siquieros, David Alfaro
Mexican Painter
1896-1974

sih-**kay**-rohs

Sisley, Alfred
French Painter
1839-1899

siz-lee
(Popular. More
correct is 'sees-lay')

Siza, Álvaro
Portuguese Architect
1933-

see-zah, **ahl-**vah-roh

Soulages, Pierre
French Painter
1919-

soo-lahz

Soutine, Chaim
French (b. Lithuania) Painter
1893-1943

soo-teen

Steichen, Edward
American Photographer
1879-1973

st(eye)k-ehn

Stella, Frank
American Painter
1936-

stell-la

Stieglitz, Alfred
American Photographer
1864-1946

shtee-glitz

Still, Clyfford
American Painter
1904-1980

stil

Sugai, Kumi   soo-**gah**-ee
Japanese (act. France) Artist
1919-1996

Talbot-Fox, William Henry **tahl**-bot fox
English Photographer
1800-1877

Tanabe, Takao   tah-**nah**-bay
Canadian Painter
1926-

Tange, Kenzo   tahn-gay
Japanese Architect
1913-

Tanguy, Yves   tahn-ghee
American (b. France) Painter
1900-1955

Tàpies, Antonio   tah-pee-ehs
Spanish Painter
1923-

Tatlin, Vladimir   taht-leen
Russian Painter, Architect
1855-1953

Tchelitchev, Pavel
American (b. Russia) Painter
1898-1957

chuh-lee-chehf

Teniers, David
Flemish Painter
1910-1990

tuh-**neers**

Ter Borch, Gerard
Dutch Painter
1617-1681

tuhr **bawrk**

Terragni, Giuseppe
Italian Architect
1904-1943

tair-**ahn**-yee

Tiepolo, Giambattista
Italian Painter
1696-1770

tee-**ehp**-oh-loh

Tinguely, Jean
Swiss Sculptor
1925-1991

ta(n)-guh-lee

Tintoretto
(Jacopo Robusti)
Italian Painter
1581-1594

tin-toh-**reh**-toh

Tissot, James
French Painter
1836-1902

tee-soh

Titian
(Titiano Vecellio)
Italian Painter
c.1485-d.1576

tish-ahn

Toulouse-Lautrec, Henri de too-looz loh-trek
French Painter
1865-1901

Tschumi, Bernard
Swiss-born Architect
1944- (act. Paris,NY)

tshoo-mee

Twombly, Cy
American Painter
1928-

twahm-blee

Uccello, Paolo
Italian Painter
1397-1475

oo-**chehl**-loh

Utrillo, Maurice
French Painter
1883-1955

ew-tree-yoh*
(*yew-trihl-loh popular
and O.K.)

Utzon, Jorn
Danish Architect
1918-

uht-zhon, yorn

Vallotton, Félix
French (b. Switzerland) Painter
1865-1925

vah-loht-to(n)

Vasarely, Victor
French (b. Hungary) Painter
1908-1997

vah-zah-**ray**-lee

Vasari, Giorgio
Italian Painter, Architect
1511-1574

vah-**zah**-ree

Vaux, Calvert
American (bEngland) Landscape Architect
1824-1895

vox
(Don't frenchify
to 'voh')

Velázquez, Diego
Spanish Painter
1599-1660

vay-**lahs**-keth

Vermeer, Jan
Dutch Painter
1632-1675

vehr-**mayr**

Veronese, Paolo
Italian Painter
1528-1588

vair-roh-**neh**-zeh

Verrocchio, Andrea del
Italian Sculptor
1435-1488

vair-**roh**-kee-yoh

**Viera da Silva,
Maria Elena**
Portuguese (act. France) Artist
1908-

vyay-rah dah **seel-**
vah

Vigée-Lebrun, Élisabeth
French Painter
1755-1842

vee-zhay luh-bruh(n)

Vignelli, Massimo
Italian Designer
1931-

veen-**yehl**-lee

Vignola, Giacomo
Italian Architect
1507-1573

vee-**nyoh-**lah

Villon, Jacques
French Painter
1875-1963

vee-yoh(n)

Vouet, Simon

voo-ay

French Painter
1590-1649

Vuillard, Édouard

vwee-yahr

French Painter
1868-1941

Warhol, Andy

wawr-hohl

American Painter
1928-1987

Watteau, Jean-Antoine

vah-toh

French Painter
1864-1921

Weegee

wee-jhee

(Arthur Fellig)
American (b. Poland) Photographer
1899-1968

Weyden, Rogier van der

v(eye)-duhn

Flemish Painter
1399-1464

Wit, Jacob de

viht

Dutch Painter
1695-1754

Witz, Conrad
German Painter
c.1400-1446

vihts

Wyeth, Andrew
American Painter
1917-

w(eye)-uth

Zadkine, Ossip
French (b. Russia) Sculptor
1819-1967

zahd-keen

Zorach, William
American (b. Lithuania) Sculptor
1887-1966

zohr-ahk

Zurbarán, Francesco de
Spanish Painter
1598-1664

tsoor-bah-**rahn**

Museums & Galleries

Akademie der Bildenden Kunst, Vienna
ah-kah-deh-**mee** dair bihl-**dehn**-dehn koonst

Alte Pinakothek, Munich
ahlt-uh pih-nah-koh-**tehk**

Bibliothèque Nationale, Paris
bee-blee-oh-tehk nah-syoh-nahl

Borghese Gallery, Rome
bohr-**gay**-zay gallery

Boijmans Museum, Rotterdam
boy-mans museum

Centre Georges Pompidou, Paris
suh(n)-truh zhorzh pohm-pee-doo

Gemäldegalerie, Dresden
geh-**mehl**-duh-gah-lair-**ee**

Museums & Galleries

Guggenheim Bilbao Museum, Bilbao
guh-gehn-h(eye)m bil-**bow** (as in cow)

Hermitage Museum, St Petersburg
err-mih-**tazh** museum

Kaiser Friedrich Museum, Berlin
k(eye)-zer **freed**-rihķ mew-**seh**-uhm

Kunsthistorisches Museum, Vienna
koonst-hihs-**tohr**-ish-uh mew-**seh**-uhm

Musée du Louvre Paris
mew-zay dew loov-ruh

Mauritshuis Gallery, The Hague
moh-**rihts**-hows gallery

Musée national de l'Orangerie, Paris
mew-zay nah-syohn-ahl duh loh-rah(n)-zuh-ree

Museums & Galleries

Musée d'Orsay, Paris
mew-zay dohr-say

Musée du Jeu de Paume, Paris
mew-zay doo zhuh duh paum

Neue Gallerie New York
noy-uh gal-ahr-**ee**

Neue Pinakothek, Munich
noy-uh pihn-ah-koh-**tehk**

Pitti Palace, Florence
pee-tee palace

Prado Museum, Madrid
prah-doh museum

Rijksmuseum, Amsterdam
r(eye)ks-myoo-zee-uhm

Museums & Galleries

Saatchi Gallery, London
sah-chee gallery

Staatliche Museum, Berlin
shtaht-lihk-uh mew-**seh**-uhm

Staatsgalerie, Stuttgart
shtahts-gah-lair-**ee**

Stedelijk Museum, Amsterdam
sted-uh-lehyk museum

Tyssen-Bornemisza Museum, Madrid
tew-sin bohr-neh-**mee**-zah museum

Uffizi Gallery, Florence
oo-**fee**-see gallery

Vitra Design Museum, Berlin
vee-trah design museum

Abbreviations, Acronyms, Variations

A.G.O
Art Gallery of Ontario, Toronto

Bilbao (bil-**bow** {as in cow})
The Guggenheim Museum,Bilbao, Spain

Beaubourg (boh-boorg)
Centre Georges Pompidou, Paris

D.I.A
Detroit Institute of Art, Detroit

Dia (**dee**-ah)
Dia Art Foundation, New York

LACMA
Los Angeles County Museum of Art

Abbreviations, Acronyms, Variations

Met
Metropolitan Museum of Art, New York

M.F.A
Museum of Fine Arts, Boston

MOCA   (**moh**-kah)
Museum of Contemporary Art, Los Angeles

MoMA   (**moh**-mah)
Museum of Modern Art, New York

ROM   (rawm)
Royal Ontario Museum, Toronto

V & A
Victoria & Albert Museum, London

Terms

Art Nouveau	ahr noo-voh
Arte Povera	ahr-teh **pov**-eh-rah
Baroque	bah-**rohk**
Bas-relief	bah ruh-leef
Bauhaus	**bow**(as in cow)-hows
Belle Époque	bell ay-pohk
Beaux Arts	boh-zahr
Byzantine	**bihz**-uhn-teen
Celtic	**kel**-tik
Chiaroscuro	kee-**yah**-roh-**skoo**-roh

Terms

Chinoiserie	shee-nwah-zuh-ree
Collage	koh-lahzh
Cubism	**kew**-bee-zuhm
Dada	dah-dah
Daguerréotype	dah-geh-ray-oh-t(eye)p
Découpage	day-koo-pahzh
De Stijl	duh stayl
Der Blau Reiter	dehr blow(as in cow) r(eye)-ter
Die Brücke	dee broo-kuh
Diptych	**dip**-tihk

Terms

Fauve	fohv
Feng Shui	fung **shway**
Fin-de-Siècle	fah(n) duh syeh-kleh
Fresco	**frehs**-koh
Genre Painting	jah(n)-ruh
Gouache	gwahsh
Grissaille	gre-z(eye)
Jugendstil	**yoo**-ghuhnd-steel
Mobile	**moh**-beel
Montage	moh(n)-tahzh

Terms

Nabis	nah-bee
Oeuvre	oov-ruh
Pointillism	pwan-tih-liz-uhm (point-ihl-lism is fine)
Renaissance	ruh-neh-sah(n)s
Rococo	roh-koh-koh
Romanesque	roh-mah-nesk
Ukiyo-e	yoo-kee-**oh**-ee
Vernissage	vehr-nee-sahzh

Select Works

Bacchus (Caravaggio)
bak-uhs

Bar at the Folies Bergère (Manet)
bar at the foh-lee behr-zher

Bedroom in Arles (Van Gogh)
bedroom in ahrl

Clos Pegase Winery (Graves)
kloh peh-gahs winery

Dance at the Moulin de la Galette (Renoir)
dance at the moo-lah(n) duh lah gah-leht

Death of Marat (David)
death of mah-rah

Déjeuner sur l'Herbe (Manet)
day-zhuh-nay sewr lehrb

Select Works

Garden at Giverny (Monet)
garden at jhee-vehr-nee

Giovanni Arnolfini and his Bride (Van Eyck)
joh-**vah**-nee ahr-nohl-**fee**-nee and his bride

The Grand Odalisque (Ingres)
The grand oh-dah-leesk

Guernica (Picasso)
gwehr-nee-kah

Isenheim Altarpiece (Grünwald)
ee-sehn-h(eye)m altarpiece

Judith slaying Holfernes (Gentileschi)
Judith slaying hohl-**fuhr**-nehz

La Loge (Renoir)
lah lohzh

Select Works

Laocöon and his Sons (Greek, 1st century B.C.)
lay-**ok**-oh-on

Lascaux Cave Paintings
lahs-koh cave paintings

Las Meninas (Velasquez)
lahs may-**nee**-nahs

Les Demoiselles d'Avignon (Picasso)
lay duh-mwah-zehl dav-vee-gnoh(n)
(Avignon refers to area in Madrid where prostitutes
found rather than the charming French town)

L.H.O.O.Q (Duchamp)
ehl-ahsh-oh-oh-kew
(Letters in French sound like she has a hot
bottom as in she has 'hot pants')

Madame Récamier (David)
mah-dahm ray-kahm-yay

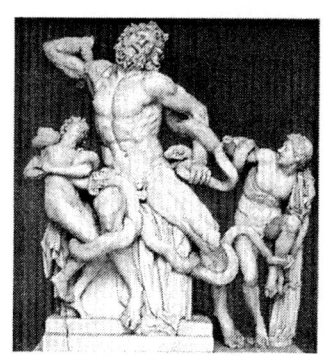

lay-**awk**-oh-awn
Laocoön (Greek)

Select Works

Mobile (Calder)
moh-beel

Mont Sainte-Victoire (Cezanne)
moh(n) sa(n)t-veek-twahr

Moulin Rouge, La Goulue (Toulouse-Lautrec)
moo-lah(n) roozh, lah goo-lew
('La Goulue'{Glutton} was the nickname of the famous
dancer portrayed)

Noli Me Tangere (Gauguin)
noh-lee meh tahn-**jehr**-eh

Notre Dame du Haut, Ronchamp (Le Corbusier)
noh-truh dahm dew oh, roh(n)-shah(n)

Personnages with Stars (Miro)
pehr-sohn-ahzh with stars

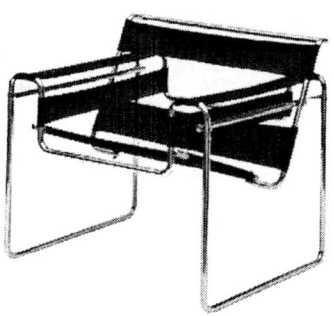

vuh-**see**-lee chair
Wassily Chair (Breuer)

Select Works

Pietà (Michelangelo)
pee-ay-**tah**

Primavera (Botticelli)
pree-mah-**vehr**-ah

Procession of the Magi (Gozzoli)
procession of the **may**-j(eye)

Sistine Ceiling (Michelangelo)
sihs-teen ceiling
(Contrary to popular belief Michelangelo did not paint
the Sistine ceiling on his back)

Sunday Afternoon on the Grand Jatte (Seurat)
Sunday afternoon on the grah(n) zhat

The Naked Maja (Goya)
the naked **mah**-hah

Select Works

The Rokeby Venus (Velasquez)
the **rohk**-bee venus

Taliesin (Frank Lloyd Wright)
tah-lee-**ess**-in
(Wright's home in Wisconsin)

Tomb of Lorenzo de'Medici (Michelangelo)
tomb of loh-**ren**-zoh day **meh**-dee-chee

Tower of Babel (Bruegel)
tower of **bay**-bul

Venus de Milo (Greek, 2nd century B.C.)
venus duh **mee**-loh
(**m(eye)**-loh acceptable)

View of Toledo (El Greco)
view of toh-**lay**-doh

Wassily Chair (Breuer)
vah-**see**-lee chair
(Created for Breuer's great friend, artist Wassily Kandinsky)

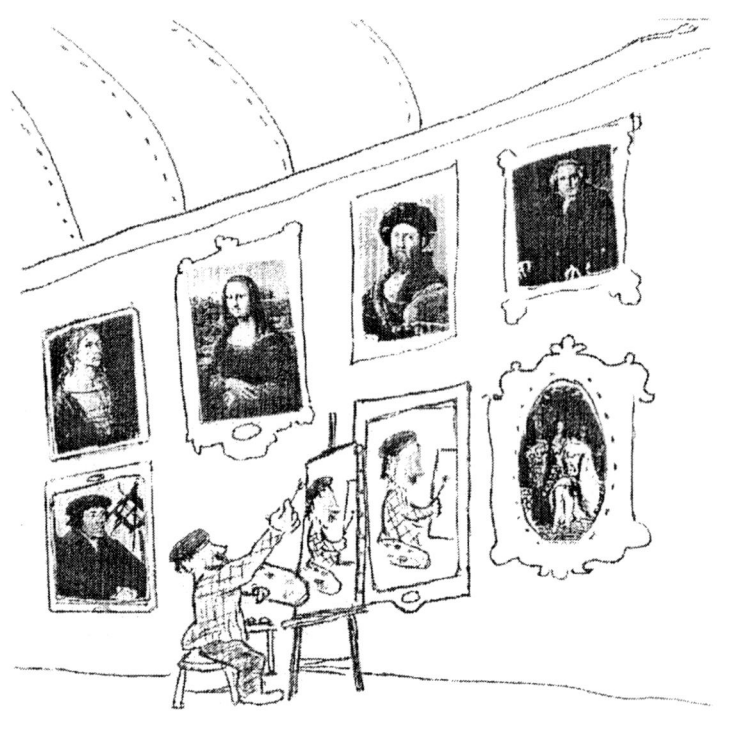

luh mew-zay dew loov-ruh
The Louvre Museum, Paris

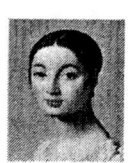

Susan Ford, an art historian and former owner of an internationally renowned architecture and design bookshop, has been active in the field of art books, both in New York and Toronto, for the past 25 years. Prior to that she was a curatorial assistant and educator at the Art Gallery of Ontario and lectured at McMaster University.

She studied at McGill University and the University of Grenoble and received her M.A. from the Institute of Fine Arts, New York University where she was a fellowship recipient.

Among other distinctions, Susan was a jury member of the Toronto Arts Awards, was among 20 select Torontonians invited to an informal discussion with Prince Charles at the Art Gallery of Toronto, and designated Alumnus Amicus by the Architecture School of the University of Toronto.

She is also tone-deaf which may account for her interest in, and concern about, pronunciation